Help the Environment

Cleaning up Litter

Charlotte Guillain

www.heinemannlibrary.co.uk
Visit our website to find out more information about Heinemann Library books.

To order:
☎ Phone 44 (0) 1865 888066
🖹 Send a fax to 44 (0) 1865 314091
🖳 Visit the Heinemann Bookshop at www.heinemannlibrary.co.uk to browse our catalogue and order online.

Heinemann Library is an imprint of Capstone Global Library Limited, a company incorporated in England and Wales having its registered office at 7 Pilgrim Street, London, EC4V 6LB – Registered company number: 6695582

Heinemann is a registered trademark of Pearson Education Limited, under licence to Capstone Global Library Limited

Editorial: Sian Smith and Cassie Mayer
Design: Philippa Jenkins
Picture research: Erica Martin, Hannah Taylor and Ginny Stroud-Lewis
Production: Duncan Gilbert

Printed and bound in China by South China Printing Co. Ltd.

ISBN 978 0 431 19216 1 (hardback)
12 11 10 09 08
10 9 8 7 6 5 4 3 2 1

ISBN 978 0 431 19222 2 (paperback)
13 12 11 10 09
10 9 8 7 6 5 4 3 2 1

British Library Cataloguing in Publication Data
Guillain, Charlotte
    Cleaning up litter. - (Help the environment) (Acorn)
    1. Litter (Trash) - Juvenile literature 2. Pollution prevention - Juvenile literature
    I. Title
    363.7'35

Acknowledgements
The publishers would like to thank the following for permission to reproduce photographs: ©Alamy pp. **5** (Gari Wyn Williams), **6**, **23 middle** (ilian), **8** (Jeff Greenberg), **4 bottom left** (Kevin Foy), **17** (Mark Boulton), **11** (Peter Glass), **4 top right**, **23 top** (Westend 61); ©ardea.com pp. **12** (Don Hadden), **14** (Valeria Taylor); ©Brand X Pixtures p. **4 bottom right** (Morey Milbradt); ©Corbis p. **22** (Philip James Corwin); ©Digital Vision p. **4 top left**; ©Getty Images p. **18** (Blend Images); ©PA Photos p. **15** (DPA Deutsche Press-Agentur, DPA); ©Photodisc pp. **7**; ©Photoeditinc. pp. **9** (Cindy Charles), **20** (Tony Freeman); ©Photolibrary pp. **19**, **23 bottom** (Bill Bachman Photography), **10** (Brandx Pictures), **21** (Deyoung Michael), **13** (Digital Vision), **16** (John Brown).

Cover photograph of a child putting litter in a bin reproduced with permission of ©Superstock (PhotoAlto). Back cover photograph of a girl picking up a bottle reproduced with permission of ©Alamy (Mark Boulton).

Every effort has been made to contact copyright holders of any material reproduced in this book. Any omissions will be rectified in subsequent printings if notice is given to the publishers.

Contents

What is the environment?

The environment is the world
all around us.

We need to care for
the environment.

What is litter?

Litter is things that we do not need any more.

Litter on the ground is bad
for the environment.

Ways to help the environment

When we pick up litter,
we are cleaning up the world.

8 We are helping the environment.

When we put litter in a rubbish
bin, we are cleaning up the world.
We are helping the environment.

If there are no rubbish bins,
we should take our litter home.

When we take our litter home,
we are cleaning up the world.
We are helping the environment.

Litter on the ground can
hurt animals.

When we pick up litter,
we are helping animals.
We are helping the environment.

Litter in the oceans can hurt animals.

When we pick up litter,
we are cleaning up the ocean.
We are helping the environment.

If glass on the ground is hit by the sun's rays, it can start a forest fire.

When we pick up glass,
we help stop forest fires.
We are helping the environment.

Some rubbish can be recycled.

When we recycle, we help to
make old things into new things.
We are helping the environment.

We can pick up litter.

We can help the environment.

How are they helping?

How are these children helping the environment?

Answer on p. 24

Picture glossary

 **environment** the world around us

 **litter** things we do not need any more

 **recycle** make old things into new things

Index

Answer to question on p.22: The children are helping the environment by recycling cans.

Note to Parents and Teachers

Before reading

Talk to children about what litter is and how it can harm the environment. For example, show them the plastic rings that hold drink cans together. Explain that these can harm animals that get caught in the rings.

After reading

• Make a class poster: Don't be a Litter Bug. On one side of the poster, glue some examples of litter that harms the environment. On the other side of the poster, draw pictures of what we can do to make less litter, such as taking litter home with us and recycling.

• Read: *What if? A Book about Recycling* by Mick Manning (Franklin Watts, 1998. ISBN: 978-0749632922).

• Sing an anti-litter song to the tune 'If you're happy and you know it'. If you see a piece of litter, pick it up. (2) You will make the world look better if you pick up all the litter. If you see a piece of litter, pick it up.